The Complete Free Cookbook

Top 30 Gluten-Free Recipes

Charlie Mason

CONTENTS

1 **Breakfast**   Pg 5

2 **Lunch**   Pg 14

3 **Dinner**   Pg 20

4 **Dessert**   Pg 29

5 **Appendix:**   Pg 37

6 **Index**   Pg 38

INTRODUCTION

Congratulations on purchasing this book and thank you for doing so.

Avoid the mistake of searching high and low, then painstakingly applying trial and error to find palatable gluten-free recipes. Look no further. This cookbook takes the mystery out of finding the most delicious, tried and true gluten-free recipes and puts them in the palm of your hand. No Muss, No fuss.

These recipes are presented in a simple, step-by-step manner to make living gluten-free simpler and more tasteful. These delectable, easy recipes are designed for busy people who want the best gluten-free meals without sacrificing a thing. Living gluten-free can seem like a daunting task. Gluten is in so many foods on the market today, so many that getting it out of your diet can be frustrating, but when you employ these recipes, you can say good riddance to gluten.

The ingredients used in these recipes are usually naturally gluten-free, but just to be sure, always check labels, especially with things like oats, broths, and chocolate, to make sure they are marked gluten-free and not prepared in a facility that has processed them alongside gluten-containing products.

Prepare your gluten-free recipes separately in containers or on surfaces that you do not use for cooking non-gluten-free meals to avoid cross-contamination.

It is recommended never to feed honey, even in cooked or pasteurized forms to children under 1 year of age.

CHAPTER 1: BREAKFAST

Gluten-Free Buttermilk Pancakes

Prep time 15 minutes, Cook time 15 minutes, about 10 servings

Ingredients:
• 1 cup fine rice flour (sifted)
• 1/3 cup potato starch
• 3 tablespoons tapioca starch
• 4 tablespoons dry buttermilk powder (you may substitute dry milk powder if you don't like the taste of buttermilk)
• 1 tablespoon sugar
• 1 1/2 teaspoons of baking powder
• ½ teaspoon of baking soda
• ½ teaspoon sea salt or kosher salt
• 1/2 teaspoon xanthan gum
• 2 cups water or milk
• 2 eggs
• 3 tablespoons canola oil

Directions:
• Combine dry ingredients in a large mixing bowl.
• Add eggs, water, and oil.
• Stir with a fork until well-mixed but still a little lumpy
• Heat a large, well-oiled griddle or large non-stick skillet to medium-high (a drop of water will sizzle when placed on the surface…just be careful it doesn't spatter on you if you test your griddle this way).
• Pour or spoon pancake batter onto the griddle and fry until bubbles form on top of the batter and edges begin to crisp up and turn golden.
• Turn pancakes over and cook until both sides are light golden-brown.
• Serve right away (or place in a warm oven at 170 degrees F if you can't serve them immediately)
• Add any toppings you desire, such as fresh fruit, fruit preserves, a dollop of Greek yogurt, butter or margarine, lightly dusted with powdered (confectioners') sugar, whipped cream, maple syrup, honey, and nuts, etc. Stir 1/8 cup of flax seeds into the mix for a

great texture and flavor. Just make sure to double-check that the toppings are all gluten-free.

Fruit and Nut Breakfast Bars

Preparation time: 10 minutes, Cook time: 20 minutes, about 8-10 Servings (12-16 bars)

Ingredients
- 1 1/4 cups blanched almond flour
- 1/4 teaspoon sea or kosher salt
- 1/4 teaspoon baking soda
- 1/4 cup grape-seed oil
- 1/4 cup agave nectar or honey
- 1 teaspoon vanilla extract
- 1/2 cup shredded or flaked coconut
- 1/2 cup hulled pumpkin seeds
- 1/2 cup hulled sunflower seeds
- 1/4 cup sliced almonds
- 1/4 cup raisins (dark, white or substitute chopped dried cranberries or apricots)

Directions:
- Preheat oven to 350 degrees Fahrenheit.
- In a separate small bowl, combine dry ingredients: almond flour, salt, and baking soda.
- In a larger mixing bowl, add liquid ingredients grapeseed oil, agave nectar (or honey) and vanilla.
- Mix all ingredients well separately, then stir the dry into the wet ingredients in the large bowl.
- Fold in coconut, pumpkin seeds, sunflower seeds, almond slices and raisins.
- Grease an 8x8 inch baking dish with the grapeseed oil (You can also experiment with using other oils such as coconut oil or non-stick cooking spray, but the grape-seed will probably still give the best result).
- Transfer the mixture to the baking pan and using moist hands, mash down evenly into the bottom of the baking pan.
- Bake for about 20 minutes or until set.
- Allow to cool, then slice into bars.

Banana-na Muffins

Preparation time: 15 minutes, Cook time: 22-25 minutes, 12 servings

Ingredients
- 2 teaspoons baking powder
- 1/4 teaspoon baking soda
- ¼ teaspoon vanilla extract
- 1/2 teaspoon xanthan gum
- 1/2 teaspoon salt
- 1/2 teaspoon cinnamon
- 1 3/4 cups pre-mixed gluten-free All Purpose flour or use Make-it-yourself All-purpose Gluten-free Flour Mix on page 33)
- 1/2 cup butter (Softened)
- 2/3 cup sugar
- 2 tablespoons molasses or honey
- 2 large eggs
- 1 1/2 cup mashed, soft, over-ripe bananas (about 2 bananas)
- 1/2 cup chopped walnuts (optional)

Directions:
- Preheat oven to 375 degrees Fahrenheit.
- Mix dry ingredients well in a small bowl: baking powder, baking soda, xanthan gum, salt, cinnamon, and flour
- In a large mixing bowl, add other ingredients a bit at a time, while mixing/stirring, butter, mashed bananas, eggs, vanilla extract, sugar, and molasses. Mix with an electric mixer on medium-high if you have one.
- Finally, fold in the walnuts a bit at a time, as you mix/stir.
- Spoon batter equally into lined muffin cups (you may also grease the muffin cups if you don't use the liners).
- Bake for 22 to 25 minutes, until the middle springs back when lightly touched or a wooden toothpick inserted into the center comes out clean.
- Let muffins sit for about 5 minutes, then serve warm or at room temperature.

Pear and Oat Scones

Preparation time: 15 minutes, Cook time: 22 minutes. 12 Servings (Serving size is 2 scones)

Ingredients
- 1 cup gluten-free oat flour
- 1 cup gluten-free oats (quick, "instant" or regular oats)
- ⅓ cup sugar
- 2 1/4 teaspoons baking powder
- 1 teaspoon cardamom (ground)
- ¼ teaspoon sea salt (finely ground)
- ⅓ cup coconut oil
- 1 large egg
- 2 tablespoons milk (any kind you prefer)
- 1 1/4 cups coarsely chopped fresh pears (remove peels if you prefer)

Directions:
- Preheat oven to 400 degrees Fahrenheit.
- Line a large cookie sheet with parchment paper or grease with coconut oil
- Add dry ingredients to a large bowl: oat flour, oats, salt, sugar, baking powder, and cardamom. Mix well.
- Separate the coconut oil into pieces and stir in a bit at a time until you have a rough-textured dough that is slightly crumbly, but will still hold together when pressed into in a ball. Adjust liquid as needed to achieve this.
- In a small bowl, whisk the egg and milk together and mix well before adding slowly to the mixture in the large bowl while stirring/mixing.
- Fold the pears into the dough until evenly distributed.
- Transfer mixture to a flat surface dusted with gluten-free oat flour. Make two patties of the mixture, about 6 inches in diameter and 1/2 inch thick. Cut each patty into 6 wedges.
- Bake wedges about an inch apart for 18 to 22 minutes, until firm and light golden-brown.
- Let cool for 5 minutes and serve warm or at room temperature.

No-Bake Peanut Butter Choco Protein Bars

Preparation Time: 20 minutes, Cook Time: 1 hour, 10 bars, about 16 grams of Protein each

Ingredients:
Bottom Layer:
- 1 1/2 cup gluten-free oat flour
- 6 dehydrated apricots
- 1/4 cup cocoa powder
- 1/4 cup brown rice syrup

Top Layer:
- 1 cup gluten-free oat flour
- ½ cup gluten-free rolled oats
- 1/2 cup gluten-free chocolate protein powder
- 1/4 teaspoon sea or kosher salt
- 1 1/2 tablespoon chia seeds
- 1 1/2 tablespoon hemp seeds
- 1/2 cup peanut butter
- 1 part flax mixture (1 tablespoon ground flax, 3 tablespoons water, mixed separately, then set aside)
- 1/4 cup honey
- ½ cup tablespoons coconut milk (shake well before using)

Topping (optional):
- 1/3 cup gluten-free chocolate chips
- 1 tablespoon sesame or flax seeds

Directions:
- Mix bottom layer ingredients in a bowl and set aside.
- In a large bowl, combine dry ingredients for the top layer and use a fork to mix well.
- Make the flax mixture: combine ground flax and water in a small bowl and stir well with a fork or whisk. Set aside and let thicken for about 5 minutes.
- Add the following to the large bowl while mixing/stirring: honey, peanut butter, coconut milk, and flax mixture from step 3, to the dry ingredients for the top layer. Mix thoroughly until uniform. Add more coconut milk as needed while mixing to form a

thick paste.
- Line an 8×8 inch metal pan with parchment paper.
- Press bottom layer mixture evenly into the bottom of the baking pan.
- Spread top layer mixture onto the bottom layer mixture.
- Refrigerate for 1 hour.
- After the bars have chilled and set, drizzle with melted chocolate sauce and sprinkle with the sesame or flax seeds (optional)
- Cut into bars.
- Keep refrigerated for up to 2 weeks.

Petite Mediterranean Quiche

Preparation time: 30 minutes, Cook time: 1 hour, Servings: 12

Ingredients:
Crust
- 2 cups of almond flour
- ½ teaspoon sea salt
- ¾ of a teaspoon of baking soda
- ¾ of a cup of coconut oil (melted)
- 1 1/2 tablespoons water

Filling
- ½ medium purple onion (diced)
- 2 garlic cloves (minced)
- 1 cup spinach (fresh or frozen-thawed and chopped)
- ½ cup diced sun-dried tomatoes in oil or dried (if dried, soak for a few minutes in warm water before dicing)
- ½ cup pitted olives (Black, green, red or a combination-sliced)
- 4 eggs
- ¼ cup of nutritional yeast (cheesy tasting deactivated yeast often sold in health food stores)
- 2 tablespoon milk or gluten-free vegetable broth
- Fresh ground black pepper to taste

Directions:
- Preheat oven to 350 degrees Fahrenheit.
- Crust: Combine dry ingredients: almond flour, salt, and baking soda. Slowly mix in ½ cup melted oil coconut and 1 1/2 tablespoons water, adding more oil as needed until mixture is

crumbly but will form a ball.

- Press crust into the muffin cups about 1/8 inch thick on the bottom and halfway up the sides. Use a fork to pierce the bottom of each crust. Bake crust 10 – 15 minutes, until lightly golden-brown.
- Filling: Sauté onions for about 3 minutes. Add garlic and spinach and Sauté for another 5 minutes.
- Remove vegetable mixture from heat and stir in sun-dried tomatoes and olives. Allow mixture to cool so that it is warm but not hot enough to cook the eggs when they are added.
- In a medium mixing bowl whisk the eggs together with the nutritional yeast, milk or vegetable broth and pepper until frothy.
- Equally spoon vegetable mixture into each crust then pour in equal amounts of the egg mixture.
- Bake 20 to 35 minutes until quiche is spongy and firm.

Bacon Cheddar Chives Scones

Preparation time: 20 minutes, Cook time: 22-25 minutes, 8 Servings

Ingredients:
Bottom of Form

- 2 cups Gluten-free All-purpose Flour or use Mix from page 33
- 1 teaspoon sea salt
- 1 tablespoon baking powder
- 2 teaspoons sugar
- 4 tablespoons butter (chilled)
- 1 cup cheddar cheese (diced or coarsely grated)
- 1/3 cup minced chives or green onion
- 1/2 pound bacon (cooked and crumbled to bits)
- 1 cup heavy cream (chilled)

Directions:
- Preheat oven to 425°F. Line cookie sheet with parchment paper.
- Combine dry ingredients: flour, salt, baking powder, and sugar. Add butter into the flour to achieve a crumbly dough, which still contains unmixed pieces of the butter.
- Add cheese, chives, and bacon until they are uniformly mixed in.
- Add ¾ cup of cream slowly while stirring. Add more cream as needed to form a thick, rough slightly sticky dough ball.

• Place dough onto a flat, gluten-free floured surface. Make a 7 inch in diameter patty about 3/4" in thickness. Cut into 8 wedges.
• Brush wedges lightly with cream
• Bake for 22 to 24 minutes. Serve warm, or at room temperature.

Yummy Breakfast Quinoa

Preparation time: 25 minutes, Cook time: 35 minutes, 8 Servings

Ingredients:
Quinoa Mixture:
• 1 cup plain quinoa (uncooked)
• 2 cups unsweetened almond milk
• 4 tablespoon honey or agave nectar
• ¼ tablespoon vanilla extract (real is best)
• 1/2 teaspoon cinnamon
• 1/4 teaspoon sea salt
• 2 eggs (beaten)
• 1/2 cup water

Filling:
• 1 cup dates (pitted and coarsely chopped)
• 1 cup water
• 1 tablespoon sugar

Topping:
• 1 ½ tablespoon coconut oil or butter (melted)
• 2 tablespoons sugar
• 1/4 cup almond flour
• 1/4 cup almonds (chopped or sliced)
• 1/4 teaspoon cinnamon
• 1 medium banana (thickly sliced)

Directions:
• Preheat your oven to 350 degrees Fahrenheit. Line or grease an 8-inch pie pan or 8X8 casserole dish.
• In a large pot, bring the almond milk to a boil. Add quinoa, vanilla, honey (or agave nectar), cinnamon and salt. Turn heat to low and cook covered for 25-30 minutes.
• Set mixture aside to cool.

- In a small saucepan, combine dates, water, and sugar. Bring to a boil and then simmer on low heat for about 15 minutes until the mixture thickens.
- In a small bowl, combine sugar, almond flour, almonds, and cinnamon. Slowly stir in the melted coconut oil or butter until it forms a crumbly streusel-like mix for the topping.
- In a large bowl, combine cooked quinoa, beaten eggs, and ½ cup water. Mix thoroughly.
- Pour half the quinoa mixture into the pie pan. Spoon date mixture on top of the first layer of quinoa and spread evenly. Spread other half of quinoa mixture on top.
- Top with uncooked banana slices, then sprinkle evenly with topping.
- Bake uncovered about 35 minutes until the mixture sets and topping is crusty and light golden-brown.
- Cool before slicing.

CHAPTER 2: LUNCH

Spinach Quinoa Bars

Preparation time: 10 minutes, Cook time 1 hour, 16 Servings

Ingredients:
- 1 cup plain uncooked quinoa
- 16 ounces frozen spinach (thawed, drained and chopped)
- 2 teaspoons extra virgin olive oil
- ¼ teaspoon garlic powder
- 1 cup nonfat cottage cheese
- 2 large eggs (beaten)
- 3 green onions (minced)
- ½ teaspoon sea salt
- ¼ teaspoon fresh ground black pepper

Directions:
- Preheat the oven to 350 degrees Fahrenheit. Line a 9 x9 inch casserole or metal baking dish with foil and lightly grease the foil.
- Bring 2 cups of water to a boil in a medium saucepan. Add quinoa and reduce heat to low. nion, avocado, and sprouts.
- Serve warm or chilled.

Simple Corn Pudding

Preparation time: 10 minutes, Cook time: 45 minutes, Serves 8

Ingredients:
- 1 red bell pepper medium (diced)
- 1 jalapeño pepper (minced-optional)
- 2 cups frozen corn (thawed)
- 1 medium onion (chopped)
- 2 tablespoons gluten-free all-purpose flour, sweet rice flour, or tapioca starch, or use mix from page 33.
- 1 teaspoon dry mustard powder
- 1 teaspoon sea salt
- ½ teaspoon fresh ground black pepper
- 2 large eggs (beaten)
- 1½ cups milk

Directions:

• Preheat the oven to 350 degrees Fahrenheit. Grease a 2-quart casserole dish with non-stick spray, butter, shortening or oil of your choice.
• In a large bowl, combine peppers, corn, onion, flour, dry mustard, salt, and pepper.
• In a small bowl, whisk together eggs and milk.
• Add egg mixture to corn mixture and mix well.
• Pour into the baking dish and bake for 45 minutes or until firm and set.

Cauliflower Curry Soup with Caramelized Onions

Preparation time: 20 minutes, Cook time: 45 minutes, 4-6 Servings

Ingredients:

• 1 large head of cauliflower (cleaned and chopped) or 2 lbs. frozen cauliflower (thawed)
• 6 tablespoons unsalted butter or coconut oil
• ½ tablespoon sugar
• 1 leek (tender white bottom part only-washed thoroughly and sliced thinly)
• 2 small onions (thinly sliced)
• 1 1/2 Tablespoons curry powder
• 1 1/2 teaspoons sea salt
• 1 Tablespoon whole cumin seeds
• 5 cups water

Directions:

• Remove outer leaves of cauliflower and any tough parts, clean and chop into bite-sized pieces. Reserve about 1 cup of cauliflower florets and slice them thinly lengthwise.
• Sauté leek, one of the onions, curry powder and salt in 3 tablespoons butter or oil for 5-7 minutes over medium-low heat until leek and onion are softened.
• Add water and cauliflower and increase heat until mixture is boiling. Reduce heat to medium-low and simmer for 30-40 minutes stirring frequently until cauliflower is tender.
• While soup is cooking, heat 3 tablespoons of oil in a medium pan over medium heat. Add onion, stir thoroughly and sprinkle

with sugar. Fry until crispy and golden brown, add cumin seeds and fry for another 1-2 minutes until the cumin seeds pop and crackle. Remove from pan and place on a paper towel.

• Reusing the pan, melt 2 tablespoons butter or oil and stir-fry reserved cauliflower florets, until tender and golden, about 6-8 minutes. Remove from heat.

• Puree soup in a blender and serve. Top each bowl of soup with stir-fried florets, toasted onions and cumin seeds.

Tremendous Taco Soup

Preparation time: 15 minutes, Cooking time: 30 minutes, Serves 4

Ingredients:
• 1 pound ground beef or turkey
• 2 tablespoons olive oil
• 1 large onion (chopped)
• 1/2 green bell pepper (chopped)
• 1 clove garlic (minced)
• 3/4 teaspoon sea salt
• 1 teaspoon cumin powder
• 1 teaspoon paprika
• 1/2 teaspoon oregano
• 1/2 teaspoon sugar
• 1 cup water
• 2 cups corn (frozen)
• 1-14 ounce can of kidney beans (rinsed and drained)
• 1-14 ounce can of black beans (rinsed and drained)
• ½ cup chopped green chilies
• 2-14 ounce cans diced tomatoes

Directions:
• In a large cooking pot, brown meat, onion, and bell pepper in the olive oil. Drain fat.
• Add spices, sugar, and water. Bring mixture to a boil.
• Add remaining ingredients: corn, garlic, beans, tomatoes, and chilies. Return to boiling, stirring frequently.
• Reduce heat, cover and simmer on low heat for at least 30 minutes.

Chicken Quesadilla

Preparation time: 15 minutes, Cooking time: 45 minutes, Serves 4

Ingredients:
- Quesadilla
- 1 pound boneless, skinless chicken breast
- 8 ounces grated pepper-jack cheese
- 8-6 inch gluten-free tortillas
- Sea salt and fresh ground black pepper to taste
- Sour cream (as a condiment)
- Pico de Gallo
- 4 cups of ripe yet firm tomatoes (diced)
- 4 sprigs of fresh cilantro (chopped)
- 1 small onion or half a medium onion (diced)
- Juice of 1 fresh lime
- 1/8 teaspoon sea salt
- 1/8 teaspoon garlic powder (or to taste)

Directions:
Pico de Gallo (may be prepared ahead of time—best served chilled)

- Place tomatoes in a bowl and drain any excess juice from tomatoes.
- Squeeze in lime juice to taste.
- Gently stir in salt, garlic powder, onion, and cilantro until the ingredients are evenly distributed.

Quesadilla
- Preheat griddle or extra-large pan to medium-high heat.
- Season chicken with salt and pepper
- Pan fry the chicken breasts about 4-5 minutes per side. Transfer the chicken to a cutting board and slice or tear into strips.
- Using the same pan or griddle, on medium-low heat, place up to 4 tortillas in the pan and distribute chicken and cheese (if you don't have a big enough pan, you will have to cook them separately.)
- Place some cheese on the tortilla evenly, then chicken, then cheese. When cheese begins to melt, cover each quesadilla with a second tortilla and flip. Repeat the process until both sides of tortillas are light golden-brown.

• As quesadillas begin to cool, slice into wedges.

Pico de Gallo

• Serve quesadillas warm with chilled Pico de Gallo and a dollop of sour cream.Cover and cook for about 15 minutes, until water is absorbed and quinoa is cooked but not mushy.

• In a large mixing bowl, place cooked quinoa. Drain any excess liquid from spinach and add to the bowl mix in oil, cottage cheese, beaten eggs, green onions, salt, garlic powder, and pepper. Stir until well blended.

• Spread mixture evenly in the prepared baking pan.

• Bake for about 1 hour, until firm and light golden-brown.

• Allow to cool thoroughly before slicing into 16 bars.

• Keep refrigerated. Serve chilled or warmed.

Nirvana Quinoa Bowl

Preparation time: 5 minutes, Cook time: 10 minutes, Serves 1

Ingredients:

• 6 eggs (beaten) or 4 ounces extra firm tofu (chopped)
• ½ cup chopped bok choy, broccoli or broccolini
• ¼ cup cherry tomatoes (halved)
• ¼ cup mushrooms (sliced)
• 1 cup kale (chopped)
• ½ cup carrot (diced or grated)
• ½ teaspoon curry powder
• ¼ teaspoon garlic powder
• ¼ teaspoon onion powder
• ¼ teaspoon paprika
• ¼ teaspoon dried basil
• ¼ teaspoon sea salt
• A pinch of red pepper flakes (optional-to taste)
• 1/8 teaspoon or a pinch of ground black pepper or white pepper (to taste)
• 1 lime (halved)
• ½ cup cooked quinoa
• ¼ avocado (sliced)
• 1 green onion (optional-washed, chopped in thirds, then cut into thin strips lengthwise)
• ¼ cup alfalfa sprouts or bean sprouts   *both are naturally

gluten-free, but make sure they are gluten-free and not grown alongside wheatgrass (washed and drained)

Directions:

• Heat pan to medium-high with a small amount of coconut or olive oil.

• In a small bowl, whisk eggs together with a small amount of oil (optional).

• When the oil is hot, add broccoli and carrots, and ½ teaspoon water. Sauté for 3-5 minutes until become tender.

• Reduce heat to medium and add kale, tomatoes, and spices. Add more water as needed and cook for about 3 minutes or until greens are wilted. Squeeze in the juice of half a lime and pour in the egg mixture. Allow the eggs to begin to congeal, then fold them into the mixture and cook until firm and crumbly. For tofu, add the tofu to vegetables and lightly brown or heat to preferred doneness.

• Place quinoa in serving bowl, top with vegetable/egg-or tofu mixture and garnish with green o

CHAPTER 3: DINNER

Treat Yourself Chicken and Dumplings

Preparation time: 15 minutes, Cook time: 1 hour and 20 minutes, Serves 6

Ingredients:
- 1 whole chicken
- 6-8 cups water
- 1 onion (chopped)
- 2 tablespoon olive or canola oil
- 2 bay leaves
- 5 carrots (sliced)
- 3 stalks of celery (sliced)
- 1/2 teaspoon fresh ground black pepper
- 1 teaspoon dried parsley
- Dumplings:
- 2 1/4 cups All-purpose gluten-free flour (or use the recipe on page 33)
- 1/4 teaspoon xanthan gum (omit if your flour has gum added)
- 2 teaspoons baking powder
- 1/2 teaspoon sea salt
- 2 eggs (beaten)
- 1 cup gluten-free chicken broth

Directions:
Stock and Chicken:

- Put the whole chicken into a large stockpot, add the bay leaves and about 6-8 cups of water (Chicken should be covered with water).
- Bring to the boil and then simmer covered for about an hour. Using a large spoon, skim the top of the water to remove foam as needed to prepare the chicken stock.
- While the chicken stock is simmering, prepare the vegetables.
- After the chicken has been cooking for about 50 minutes, remove the chicken from the pot and set aside to cool.
- Remove the bay leaves from the chicken stock. Heat oil in a second pot (large enough to accommodate the broth, chicken stock, and dumplings). Sauté the onion, carrots, and celery for about five minutes.

- Add the chicken stock to the pan with the vegetables on low heat and continue to simmer.
- When the chicken has cooled enough to handle, remove the skin. Remove the meat from the chicken manually and add to the pot with the vegetables and stock.

Dumplings:
- To make the dumplings add the dry ingredients: gluten-free flour mix, baking powder and salt to a large mixing bowl.
- In a separate bowl, whisk together the chicken broth, eggs, and parsley until they are well-mixed.
- Then add the egg mixture to the dry ingredients and mix well until you have a thick, soft, sticky dough mixture.
- Take heaping teaspoons of the dough and drop them into the stock, taking care to keep them relatively similar in size.
- Cover and simmer for 20 more minutes until the dumplings are firm and holding together well.

Slow Cooker Paella

Preparation time: 10 minutes, Cook time: 4 hours, Serves 6-8

Ingredients:
- 8 ounces of gluten-free chorizo, chicken or pork sausage (browned and sliced)
- 1 pound chicken (cooked and cubed)
- 16 ounces frozen seafood mix (such as shrimp, scallops, and mussels, etc.)
- 1½ cups (dry) long grain brown rice
- 1½ cups gluten-free chicken broth
- 1 medium onion (chopped)
- ½ cup fennel (optional-chopped)
- 1 medium bell pepper (chopped)
- 2 cups diced canned tomatoes with juice
- 1 cup frozen green peas
- 1 teaspoon ground turmeric
- ½ teaspoon ground paprika
- 1½ teaspoons garlic salt
- lemon wedge and fennel sprigs to garnish

Directions:

- In skillet, heat oil. Brown the chicken and sausage for 5-7 minutes, then remove, cool and chop.
- Add the chicken, rice, onion, fennel (optional), bell pepper, tomatoes, broth, salt, and spices to the slow cooker, and mix to combine.
- Cook on high for 3½ hours, then stir.
- Under cold running water, thaw seafood and peas, then mix the seafood and the peas in into the slow cooker and continue to cook on high for another 30 minutes.
- Stir well, garnish with a lemon wedge and serve warm.

Savory Thai Coconut Chicken

Ingredients:

- 2 teaspoons vegetable oil
- 2 shallots (sliced)
- 2 tablespoons gluten-free Thai green curry paste
- 1 large red bell pepper (julienned)
- 1 cup gluten-free chicken broth
- 1 tablespoon cornstarch
- 1 cup coconut milk (shaken well)
- 1 tablespoon sugar
- 1 tablespoon gluten-free fish sauce
- 1 teaspoon gluten-free tamari or gluten-free soy sauce
- 1 pound boneless, skinless chicken thighs (cut into 1-inch pieces)
- 12 ounces frozen sugar snap peas
- 2 tablespoons fresh lime juice
- 4 cups brown rice (cooked)
- 2 sprigs fresh basil (cut thinly lengthwise)

Directions:

- Heat oil in a large pan. Stir in the curry paste. Add Shallots. Stir-fry at medium-high for about 3 minutes or until the shallots begin to soften and become more translucent. Add bell pepper. Cook for about 2 minutes more.
- In a small bowl, whisk together 1/4 cup of the broth and the cornstarch. Allow 5 minutes to thicken.
- Add remaining broth, coconut milk, sugar, fish sauce and gluten-free soy sauce or tamari to the skillet. Heat to boiling over medium-high heat. Add chicken and frozen peas; return to boiling. Cook 8

minutes stirring frequently until chicken is done. Stir in cornstarch mixture and stir continuously, cooking about 2 more minutes until mixture has thickened. Stir in lime juice.
- Spoon warm cooked rice into bowls, and spoon curry on top. Garnish with fresh basil.

Crispy Orange Chicken

Prep time: 15 minutes Cook time: 15 minutes Yield: 4 servings

Ingredients:

Sauce:
- ¾ cup of orange juice (no pulp)
- 2 tablespoons vinegar
- ¾ cup of gluten-free chicken broth
- 2 tablespoons of cornstarch or sweet white rice flour
- ¼ cup of tamari or gluten-free soy sauce
- ½ teaspoon of garlic powder
- ¼ teaspoon of red pepper flakes (optional)
- ¼ teaspoon of powdered ginger
- 3 tablespoons of honey

Chicken:
- 1 1/2 pounds chicken breast (skinned, de-boned and cubed)
- 1 1/2 cups gluten-free cornflakes corn-flakes (crushed).

Serving:
- 3 cups cooked Jasmine or Basmati white rice
- chopped green onions (for garnish)

Directions:
- Preheat the oven to 350 degrees Fahrenheit. Line an appropriately large cookie sheet with parchment paper.
- In a saucepan, combine orange juice, chicken broth, and flour. Whisk briskly to mix. Add rice vinegar, soy sauce or tamari, vinegar, garlic powder, red pepper flakes, ginger, and honey.
- Place the saucepan over medium-high heat. Simmer, stirring frequently. About 5 minutes or until sauce thickens. Remove the

sauce from the heat and transfer it to a large bowl. Allow the sauce to cool, whisking occasionally, until cooled. The sauce can also be made beforehand and refrigerated.
- Place about 1/2 of the sauce in a separate, medium-size bowl.
- Dip raw chicken cubes individually into the sauce, then into the crumbs and arrange on a baking sheet about ½ inch apart.
- Bake for about 15 minutes or until golden brown on all sides.
- Remove from the oven and toss the chicken into the remaining sauce.
- Serve over rice. Garnish with fresh green onions if desired.

Cozy Cottage Pie

Preparation time: 15 minutes, Cook time: 1 hour, Serves 6

Ingredients:
- 1 pound lean ground lamb, Turkey or beef
- 1 tablespoon oil
- 3 large carrots (diced)
- 1 large onion (diced)
- 2 tablespoons tomato paste
- 1 cup frozen green peas
- 1 tablespoon gluten-free Worcestershire sauce or gluten-free Fish Sauce
- 2 cups gluten-free beef stock
- 4 medium potatoes peeled (cubed)
- 2 tablespoons butter or margarine
- 2 tablespoons arrowroot (powdered) or cornstarch
- 1/2 cup shredded sharp cheddar cheese or ¼ cup nutritional yeast (optional)
- 1/8 teaspoon sea salt (or adjust to taste)
- 1/8 teaspoon freshly ground black pepper (or adjust to taste)

Directions:
- Heat the oil in a pan. Add onion and carrots and sauté for a 3 - 4 minutes.
- Add meat and brown over medium heat, stirring frequently. Drain off fat. Add the tomato purée and Worcestershire or fish sauce and continue to cook more minutes. Add frozen peas and beef stock. Stir well to mix and reduce heat to medium-low. Cover and simmer for about 20 minutes.

- Prepare potatoes: In a large pot, cover potatoes with water and bring to a boil. Lower heat cook over medium-high heat for about 20 minutes until potatoes are soft enough to be easily pierced with a fork.
- Remove potatoes from heat and drain.
- Add butter or margarine, salt, and pepper to taste. If using the nutritional yeast, add that now and stir. If desired, you can add a small amount of milk (about 1-2 tablespoons). Mash potatoes with a masher, fork or whisk. Alternatively, you can mix from low in the beginning, increasing to whip at the end, with an electric mixer until you achieve a creamy but still slightly lumpy potato mixture.
- Preheat oven to 350 degrees Fahrenheit.
- Remove the cover of the pan with the meat-vegetable mixture and cook uncovered for 20 more minutes, stirring occasionally.
- Add the arrowroot powder or the cornstarch to a small bowl with about 3 tablespoons of water (cold) and whisk briskly.
- Remove pan from heat and move the meat and vegetables aside with a spoon to expose an area of the liquid broth. Slowly add the starch mixture to the exposed are while whisking continuously until the broth begins to thicken. Stir the mixture well to combine. If the liquid is not thick enough, add more starch by the same method until desired thickness is achieved.
- Put the prepared meat mixture into a casserole or pie dish. Top with mashed potatoes and spread them out evenly to form a "crust." Top with cheddar cheese (optional)
- Bake for 20-25 minutes until potatoes are light golden-brown. You may also broil on high for the last couple of minutes to brown the top and cheese if desired.

Stuffed Squash with Quinoa

Preparation time: 20 minutes, Cook time: 40 minutes, Serves 4

Ingredients:
2 acorn (or similar small winter squash--halved and de-seeded)

- 1 tablespoon extra-virgin olive oil
- 8 ounces Shiitake or Baby Portabella mushrooms (chopped)
- 1 medium onion (diced)
- 1-2 tablespoons fresh rosemary (finely chopped-or substitute 1 teaspoon dried rosemary)

- 1/2 cup dried cranberries
- 1 1/2 cups plain quinoa (cooked)

Directions:
- Preheat oven to 400 degrees Fahrenheit.
- Line a cookie sheet with foil, grease, and salt the foil lightly with oil of your choosing, place squash cut side down on the pan.
- Bake for 30 minutes.
- Meanwhile, cook the quinoa.
- While the quinoa and squash are cooking, heat olive oil in a large skillet or pan, over medium-high heat. Sauté onions and mushrooms for 5-7 minutes. Drain off excess liquid. Stir in the rosemary and cook an additional 2-3 minutes. Remove from heat and drain off any excess liquid.
- Transfer the vegetables to a large mixing bowl. Add cooked quinoa and cranberries. Stir well to combine. Set aside.
- Once the squash can be easily pierced with a fork, remove from oven and spoon the onion and quinoa mixture into each squash half in equal portions.
- Serve warm.

Lime and Cilantro Chicken over Cauliflower "Rice"

Preparation time: 20 minutes, Cook time: 29 minutes, Serves 4

Ingredients:

Chicken:
- 1 pound skinned, deboned chicken breast
- 1/4 cup fresh lime juice
- 2 tablespoons extra-virgin olive oil
- 1/3 cup fresh cilantro (minced)
- 2 cloves fresh garlic (minced) or substitute ½ teaspoon dry garlic powder
- 1/8 teaspoon sea salt
- 1/2 teaspoon honey

Cauliflower "rice"
2 tablespoons extra-virgin olive oil
- 3 cups cauliflower (riced or minced in a food processor if you cannot find premade cauliflower "rice")
- 2 teaspoons garlic powder
- 1 teaspoon ground cumin
- 1/8 sea salt
- 1/2 cup black beans (rinsed and drained)
- 1/4 cup purple onion (uncooked, diced or thinly sliced)

Toppings:
- 1 cup ripe cherry tomatoes (halved or quartered)
- 1 avocado (quartered or thinly sliced)

Directions:
Chicken:
- Heat olive oil in a large skillet over medium heat.
- Lightly brown chicken over medium heat for 5-8 minutes on each side.
- Remove chicken from heat and slice or tear into strips when cool enough to do so.
- Place the chicken strips in a bowl. Add cilantro, garlic, salt, lime juice and honey. Mix well and set aside.

Cauliflower:
- Heat oil in a large skillet. Add cauliflower and spices. Sauté on medium heat for about 5 minutes. Add black beans and stir-fry for 2-3 minutes longer or until all ingredients are evenly warmed. Add raw onion and mix well.
- Place rice mixture in a bowl, top with chicken mixture, then garnish each bowl with avocado and cherry tomatoes.

Country Style Pork Chops

Preparation time: 12 minutes, Cooking time: 30 minutes, Serves 6

Ingredients:
- 2 eggs (large, beaten)
- 2 tablespoons milk
- 5 cups cornflake cereal (crushed makes about 2 cups)

- 6 boneless pork chops (3/4 inches thick)
- 1/4 teaspoon dried thyme
- ¼ teaspoon dried rosemary
- 1 teaspoon sea salt
- 1 teaspoon garlic powder
- ¼ teaspoon fresh ground black pepper

Directions:
- Preheat oven to 350 degrees Fahrenheit.
- Quickly whisk together eggs and milk a wide, shallow bowl.
- Place cornflake crumbs on a separate plate.
- Rub pork chops with spices.
- Dip pork chops in egg mixture, then lightly press into the cornflake crumbs until evenly coated.
- Place pork chops on a greased baking sheet.
- Bake for 30 to 35 minutes or until desired doneness is achieved.

CHAPTER 4: DESSERT

Flourless Chocolate Cake

Preparation time: 20 minutes, Cook time: 25 minutes, Serves 8-12

Ingredients:
Cake:

- 1 cup dark or semi-sweet chocolate chips
- 1 teaspoon vanilla extract
- 1/2 cup unsalted butter
- 3/4 cup granulated sugar
- 1/4 teaspoon salt
- 3 eggs (large)
- 1/2 cup unsweetened gluten-free cocoa powder
- 2 teaspoons espresso powder (optional)

Glaze:
1 cup dark or semi-sweet chocolate chips
1/2 cup heavy cream

Directions:
Cake:
- Preheat oven to 375 degrees Fahrenheit. Grease an 8" round cake pan; cut a piece of parchment paper to fit, grease it, and place in the bottom of the pan. A spring-form cake pan also works well.
- Melt chocolate and butter in a microwave-safe bowl. Stir.
- Add chocolate mixture to a mixing bowl. Stir in sugar, salt, espresso powder (optional) and vanilla.
- Add eggs. Stir. Add cocoa powder and mix well.
- Spoon the batter into the prepared pan.
- Bake the cake for 25-30 minutes
- Remove from the oven and allow to cool for several minutes.
- Take a butter knife or nylon spatula around the edges to loosen them and flip the cake upside down onto a plate. Allow cake to cool completely before glazing.

Glaze:

• Place the chocolate and cream a bowl microwave and heat until hot but not bubbling (about 2-3 minutes depending on your microwave). Continue to heat and stir until chocolate is melted and well-incorporated into a smooth liquid glaze.

• Drizzle glaze over the cake with a spoon. Allow glaze to set up before serving. It may be refrigerated to help with the process.

Sweetest Lemon Drizzle Cake

Preparation time: 15 minutes, Cooking time: 50 minutes, Serves 8-12

Ingredients:
Cake:
• 1 cup all-purpose gluten-free flour (or use recipe on page 33)
• 1 cup oil
• 1/3 cup almond flour
• 2 tablespoons poppy seeds (optional)
• 2 teaspoons baking powder
• 1/2 teaspoon xanthan gum
• 1 1/3 cups sugar
• 1 teaspoon vanilla extract
• 4 eggs (large)
• 1 lemon (grate zest and juice)

Glaze:
• 1 cup confectioners' sugar
• 1/4 cup fresh lemon juice

Directions:
Cake:
• Preheat oven to 350 degrees Fahrenheit. Grease and flour a 5x9 inch loaf pan.

• Combine dry ingredients in a small mixing bowl: flour, almond flour, poppy seeds (optional), baking powder and xanthan gum. Mix well.

• In a medium mixing bowl, combine olive oil, sugar, and vanilla. Mix well. Add eggs and mix well. Stir in the zest and juice from the lemon. Add the flours and other dry ingredients slowly while stirring the egg mixture. Continue until well mixed.

• Pour batter into loaf pan and bake for about 50 minutes until top is lightly browned and a toothpick will come out clean when stuck in the center and pulled out.

• Allow the cake to cool. Make sure it is completely cooled before removing it from the loaf pan to put on the glaze.

Glaze:

• Add confectioners' sugar to a small bowl. Whisk in lemon juice slowly until you have achieved a smooth glaze.

• Remove cooled cake from loaf pan and place on a serving plate.

• Use a spoon to drizzle glaze over the top of the cake.

• Allow glaze to set fully before slicing and serving. You may garnish with a few ripe red raspberries or a sprig of fresh mint if desired.

Scrumptious Apple Crisp

Preparation time: 15 minutes, Cook time: 25-30 minutes, Serves 8

Ingredients:

• 4 cups baking apples, i.e., Granny Smith (sliced and peeled)
• 1 tablespoon of sugar
• 1 teaspoon cornstarch
• 2 teaspoons ground cinnamon
• 2 tablespoons water
• 1 pinch nutmeg (optional)
• 1/2 cup almond flour
• 1/2 cup gluten-free regular oats
• 1/4 cup (packed) brown sugar
• 2 tablespoons unsalted butter (softened)

Directions:

• Preheat the oven to 350 degrees Fahrenheit. Grease 9x12 inch baking dish.

• In a large bowl, combine apples, sugar, water, cornstarch, half the cinnamon, and nutmeg (optional).

• Mix well.

• In a small mixing bowl, add almond flour, oats, brown sugar, half the cinnamon, and butter. Stir until a crumbly, streusel-like mixture is achieved.

• Place the apple filling in the prepared baking dish.

The Complete Gluten-Free Cookbook

- Sprinkle the topping evenly over the filling.
- Bake for 25 to 30 minutes.
- Serve warm or at room temperature.

Dark Chocolate Toffee Candy

Preparation time: 10 minutes, Cook time: 20 minutes, About 24 pieces

Ingredients:
Bottom of Form

- 1 cup unsalted butter
- 1/2 teaspoon sea salt
- 1 1/2 cups sugar
- 3 tablespoons water
- 1 tablespoon clear (light) corn syrup
- 2 cups chopped pecans or sliced almonds (toasted)
- 2 2/3 cups semisweet or bittersweet chocolate chips

Directions:
- Melt butter in a large saucepan over medium-low heat.
- Add salt, sugar, water, and corn syrup, stirring frequently.
- Bring to a boil.
- Continue to simmer for about 10-12 minutes without stirring until the mixture thickens and darkens. It should reach 300 degrees Fahrenheit on a candy thermometer. (If you don't have a thermometer, drop a spoonful into ice water. Take the piece out and check to see that it is brittle enough to be cracked, not gummy or chewy.
- Spread half the nuts in an even layer on a lightly greased baking sheet. Top them with half the chocolate.
- Pour the prepared syrup quickly over the nuts and chocolate chips. Distribute evenly. Top right away with the remaining chocolate chips and nuts.
- Allow to set for about 7 minutes, then depress the mixture with a spatula.
- While the candy is still slightly warm, loosen from the baking sheet.
- When completely cooled, snap the candy into bite-sized chunks.
- Store in an airtight container.

Most Delightful Victoria Sandwich Cake

Preparation time: 20 minutes, Cooking time: 15 minutes, Serves 8

Ingredients:

Cake:
- 3/4 cup margarine
- 3/4 cup casters' (finely granulated white sugar, not powdered or confectioners') sugar
- 2 eggs
- 1/2 teaspoon vanilla extract
- 3/4 cup All-purpose gluten-free flour (or use mix on page 33)
- 3 tablespoons milk

Buttercream:
- ½ cup confectioner's sugar
- 1/4 cup margarine
- ½ teaspoon vanilla extract
- Note: you will need about ½ cup raspberry jam (preserves) also.

Directions:
- Preheat the oven to 375 degrees Fahrenheit. Prepare 2 8 inch cake pans.
- In a large mixing bowl, add cake margarine and casters' sugar. Mix well until they are well blended and creamy. Stir in eggs and cake vanilla. Mix well.
- Stir in flour and baking powder, mixing well.
- Slowly add the milk while stirring until you achieve a pourable liquid batter and all ingredients are well incorporated.
- Bake for about 15-18 minutes or until a wooden toothpick can be inserted into the centre and comes out clean.
- Buttercream: In a small mixing bowl, add sugar and margarine. Using a fork, whisk, or electric mixer on whip, cream margarine and sugar until it becomes creamy and airy.
- Flip the cakes out onto a cooling rack.
- When cake is completely cool, place one layer on a cake serving plate.
- Spread the layer evenly with jam.
- Spread the buttercream evenly over the jam, then place the top

layer.
• Dust the top of the cake with powdered sugar and garnish with fresh raspberries if desired.

Decadent Chocolate-Caramel Shortbread

Preparation time: 15 minutes, Cooking time: 15-20 minutes, Makes 40 pieces

Ingredients:
• 1 ½ cups butter
• ¾ cup sugar
• 2 cups gluten-free self-rising flour

Caramel:
• 1 cup butter
• 1 cup sugar
• 4 tablespoons golden syrup
• 1 can (about 12 ounces) sweetened condensed milk

Topping:
• 1 ½ cups chocolate (dark, milk, white or a mix)

Directions:
• Preheat oven to 350 degrees Fahrenheit.
• Cube butter or use softened butter. Combine with the sugar. Mix until creamy.
• Add the flour and mix well until it makes a dough that will form into a crumbly dough ball.
• Press the dough evenly into a large greased and baking pan and pierce with a fork to vent evenly across the entire surface.
• Bake for 15-20 minutes until light golden in color.
• Set aside and allow to cool.
• Caramel: combine sugar, butter, syrup and condensed milk in a saucepan over low heat stirring frequently until mixed well.
• Increase heat and boil for 3-4 minutes. Then turn up the heat and boil for 3-4 minutes, stirring constantly.
• Test to see if it is the right consistency by dropping a small amount into a glass of cold water. The caramel will form a gooey, soft blob.

- Pour the caramel over the cooled base and allow to set. (about 1 hour or longer)
- Once the caramel is set, melt the chocolate and spread over the caramel. Allow to set. (1 hour or more)
- Chill in refrigerator before cutting.
- Store in an airtight container.

Heavenly Macaroons

Preparation time: 5 minutes, Cooking time: 15 minutes, 6 Servings of 2 cookies

Ingredients:
- 1 1/3 cups flaked coconut
- 1/3 cup confectioners' sugar
- 2 tablespoons rice flour
- 2 egg whites
- ½ teaspoon almond extract

Directions:
- Preheat oven to 325 degrees Fahrenheit.
- In a medium mixing bowl, mix coconut, sugar and rice flour together.
- Add the egg whites and almond extract. Mix well.
- Drop heaping tablespoons full of dough onto a well-greased cookie sheet.
- Bake for 15-18 minutes until peaks and edges are light golden-brown

Silkiest Chocolate Mousse

Ingredients:
- 1 2/3 cups heavy whipping cream
- 2 teaspoon vanilla extract
- 1/2 teaspoon sea or kosher salt (finely ground)
- 4 egg whites
- 1/2 cup sugar
- ¾ cup (6 ounces) semisweet (dark) chocolate (melted and cooled)

Directions:

- In a large bowl, whisk cream, vanilla, and salt briskly until peaks form and chill.
- In another large bowl, beat egg whites with a whisk until soft peaks form. Slowly whisk in sugar and whisk quickly until stiff peaks form.
- Fold in melted chocolate to egg whites
- Add whipped cream and mix well from step 1.
- Divide among parfait cups; chill.
- Sprinkle with chocolate shavings before serving. Garnish with chocolate shavings of your choice, such as white chocolate for contrast. You can also top with cocoa powder, red raspberries or pitted black cherries

CHAPTER 5: APPENDIX:

Make-it-yourself Gluten-Free Multi-Purpose Flour Mix

Preparation Time: 5 minutes, Makes: 18 cups

Ingredients:
- 4 ¼ cups brown rice flour
- 4 ¼ cups white rice flour
- 4 ¼ cups sweet rice flour
- 4 ¼ cups tapioca flour (or tapioca starch)
- 2 ½ tablespoons xanthan gum

Add all the ingredients to a large bowl and mix until well-blended.

Store in a cool dry place in an airtight canister or jar.

Hopefully, this cookbook has been helpful to you. We would love to hear, on Amazon, about your positive experiences with the recipes and your artistry in the kitchen.

INDEX

Chapter 1: Breakfast
- Gluten-Free Buttermilk Pancakes
- Fruit and Nut Breakfast Bars
- Banana-na Muffins
- Pear and Oat Scones
- No-Bake Peanut Butter Choco Protein Bars
- Petite Mediterranean Quiche
- Bacon Cheddar Chives Scones
- Yummy Breakfast Quinoa

Chapter 2: Lunch
- Spinach Quinoa Bars
- Simple Corn Pudding
- Cauliflower Curry Soup with Caramelized Onions
- Tremendous Taco Soup
- Chicken Quesadilla
- Nirvana Quinoa Bowl

Chapter 3: Dinner
- Treat Yourself Chicken and Dumplings
- Slow Cooker Paella
- Savory Thai Coconut Chicken
- Crispy Orange Chicken
- Cozy Cottage Pie
- Stuffed Squash with Quinoa
- Lime and Cilantro Chicken over Cauliflower "Rice"
- Country Style Pork Chops

Chapter 4: Dessert
- Flourless Chocolate Cake
- Sweetest Lemon Drizzle Cake
- Scrumptious Apple Crisp
- Dark Chocolate Toffee Candy
- Most Delightful Victoria Sandwich Cake
- Decadent Chocolate-Caramel Shortbread
- Heavenly Macaroons
- Silkiest Chocolate Mousse

Printed in Poland
by Amazon Fulfillment
Poland Sp. z o.o., Wrocław